Original title:
Tropical Garden Escape

Copyright © 2025 Creative Arts Management OÜ
All rights reserved.

Author: Rafael Sterling
ISBN HARDBACK: 978-1-80581-556-3
ISBN PAPERBACK: 978-1-80581-083-4
ISBN EBOOK: 978-1-80581-556-3

Sunlit Canopy

Under the sun where the shadows play,
Lizards dance in a snazzy ballet.
Sipping smoothies from a giant leaf,
A monkey steals my snack; oh, what a thief!

Parrots squawk tales of their latest spree,
While Lemurs plan a new updated decree.
Frogs in hats croak their favorite tunes,
As bees join in, buzzing poppy balloons.

Dew-Kissed Blossoms

In morning light, the flowers blush,
A squirrel trips in a clumsy rush.
Petals giggle as the breeze sweeps by,
While the sun dons shades, oh me, oh my!

Bees throw a party on sweet-willed thyme,
With tiny DJ bugs that groove in time.
Butterflies twirl like they've lost their mind,
In this floral disco, true joy you'll find.

Enchanted Ferns

Ferns play peek-a-boo with shy sunbeams,
Whispering secrets of their leafy dreams.
A gnome in red starts to tap his toes,
As plants debate who wears the best clothes.

With fronds that wiggle and giggle loud,
The mushrooms gather, forming a crowd.
They jest about the best soil misuse,
While sipping rainwater, their favorite juice.

Nectar and Spice

Buzzing about in a fragrant haze,
A bee forgot its dance; what a phase!
Sipping nectar from a laughing bloom,
Stealing a sweet kiss in a colorful room.

A fountain sprays water, a playful dance,
As grasshoppers jump in a wild romance.
With every drop, giggles do entice,
In a garden filled with nectar and spice.

Whispers of a Lush Oasis

In a haven bright and green,
Funny critters dance unseen,
A parrot tells a joke so grand,
While a chameleon paints the sand.

The monkeys swing in crazy glee,
Chasing shadows, wild and free,
A turtle giggles, slow but spry,
As butterflies flit and birds fly high.

Secrets Beneath the Palms

Underneath the rustling leaves,
A squirrel plot twists and weaves,
It steals a coconut with flair,
While sleeping iguanas unaware.

Secrets whispered in the breeze,
A crab finds dance moves with ease,
The lizards crack a sunny grin,
As flowers giggle, letting in.

Vibrant Colors, Silent Breezes

Painted petals wave hello,
As funny bees begin to flow,
Bumblebees in polka dots,
Sipping nectar from silly pots.

A rainbow parrot struts its stuff,
Flirting with a flower, kind of tough,
The sunbeams laugh, they act like clowns,
Chasing shadows, flipping frowns.

Lianas and Laughter

Lianas twist like curly hair,
Swinging creatures everywhere,
A toucan plays hopscotch in the rain,
While sloths play chess, isn't that insane?

Laughter bubbles up from roots,
Turtles wear the silliest boots,
The crickets chirp a comic tune,
As the sun sets high, beneath the moon.

Hidden Grove Revelations

In the grove where coconuts grow,
A monkey wearing socks steals the show.
He dances like he's on a spree,
Spinning in circles, oh, so free.

Parrots squawk their gossiping tales,
While geckos sport their colorful scales.
A lizard sips from a tiny cup,
Saying, "Cheers to this wild, silly setup!"

Lush Harmony

A sloth serenades the bees with song,
While a toucan winks and joins along.
They form a band in a leafy slot,
Playing tunes that are quirky and hot.

With every strum, the iguana claps,
And the warm breeze takes gentle naps.
Blossoms bounce, wearing silly hats,
As critters groove like overzealous cats.

Canopies of Delight

Underneath the sway of palm tree crowns,
Frogs in bow ties hop around towns.
A turtle wears shades, striking a pose,
While a sparkly beetle plays with his toes.

Sunbeams dance on the ground with glee,
As butterflies sip from lemon tea.
All creatures join in a silly chase,
Laughing and tumbling, what a wild race!

Chasing Shadows

In shadows where the sunlight plays,
A crab moonwalks in funny ways.
He drags along his sandy sack,
Waving claws with a peculiar knack.

A kadunk of laughter fills the air,
As chameleons blush without a care.
They trip on petals, slip on dew,
Painting the scene in outrageous hues.

Sun-kissed Leaves

In the sun, leaves giggle bright,
Dancing shadows, oh what a sight!
The squirrels throw a party spree,
While butterflies sip their sweet tea.

Coconuts drop with a mighty thud,
Making unsuspecting folks grudge!
It's a game of dodge and weave,
In this land, you best believe!

Hidden Paths

Winding trails with secret treats,
Where cheeky frogs wiggle their feets.
Follow the laughter of the breeze,
To stumble upon some chomping bees.

There's a sign that reads 'Watch Your Step!',
But who could heed it? Oh, what a rep!
Every turn hides a playful jest,
Each corner brings a silly quest.

The Call of the Hummingbird

Tiny dancer with wings so fast,
Zooming by like a flying blast!
Whispers sweetly to the bright blooms,
While sipping nectar, chaos looms.

With a twist and twirl, it's pure delight,
Chasing shadows, a comical flight.
Nearby, the bumblebees start to buzz,
Complaining loud, "Hey, it's all ours!"

Enchanted by the Mango Tree

Under the mango, laughter reigns,
With sticky fingers and fruity stains.
Swinging low, the branches creak,
As monkeys plan their cheeky sneak!

Those pesky fruits have rolls of fun,
Bouncing down like a fruit-filled gun.
Chasing after, slipping in glee,
Come join the frolic, wild and free!

Serenity Amidst the Ferns

Ferns wave softly in the breeze,
While turtles walk with the greatest ease.
Lizards posing in sunlit grace,
Pretend they're having a stylish race!

A sudden twitch, a rustle below,
A rabbit hops with a comical slow.
In this escape, laughter is found,
With nature's antics all around!

Secrets of the Rainforest

In the jungle, parrots chat,
Swinging monkeys wear a hat.
Lizards dance with wiggly tails,
While sloths share their sleepy tales.

Frogs hop by with tiny shoes,
Trying hard to pick their muse.
Bright toucans have quite the flair,
Like fashionistas beyond compare.

Gentle Murmurs Among the Leaves

Whispers flow from flowers' lips,
Insects jog and do their flips.
Caterpillars all in a race,
Uncle Tortoise takes his place.

Bamboo shakes with a funny creak,
As giggling squirrels play hide and seek.
Butterflies in silly prance,
Twisting like they're in a dance.

Paradise in Full Bloom

Petals yell in colors bright,
While bees buzz in pure delight.
Gazing at a coconut tree,
A parrot shouts, "Come join me!"

A cheeky gopher makes a mess,
While flowers giggle, "What a stress!"
The day's a wink, with cheek and charm,
Every critter sounds the alarm.

Abode of Exotic Wonders

Lemurs leap with endless glee,
While raccoons host a jamboree.
Coconut drinks spill on the ground,
As laughter echoes all around.

Fruit bats swing in moonlit grace,
Chasing fireflies in a race.
Nature plays its silly tune,
Underneath the glowing moon.

Gardens of Echoing Laughter

In the garden where giggles grow,
Chasing butterflies in a silly row.
A parrot laughs at my dance moves,
While a monkey sneaks in to make grooves.

The sun tickles flowers, they start to sway,
Petals gossip about the funny way.
Snakes in sunglasses slither by,
Claiming they're cooler than a flying pie.

Bees buzz jokes with a honeyed tone,
As a frog leaps high on a trampoline throne.
The laughter echoes down the leafy trails,
Where every creature dances without fails.

Reverie in the Rainforest Breeze

The leaves whistle tunes as I stroll on by,
While frogs debate who's the smartest guy.
Monkeys throw jokes like ripe coconuts,
Giggling wildly, they'll aim for my cuts.

In the misty breeze, a sloth takes a nap,
Dreaming of goldfish in a cozy lap.
A toucan sneezes, and it's quite a scene,
Splashing nectar like a sticky queen.

With every step, the ground tickles my feet,
As flowers burst into song, quite the beat.
Something bumps my leg—I glance around,
A crab in a cape mischief-bound.

Whispers of the Palms

Palms chat softly under a cheeky sky,
They giggle at squirrels rushing to fly.
Turtles wear hats, looking quite grand,
As they shuffle around on the sandy land.

Lizards in tuxedos strut with flair,
While flamingos balance with a laugh in the air.
The driftwood jokes about old wooden tales,
As the breeze carries forth their winking gales.

A coconut rolls with a comical thud,
As laughter builds like a sugar-filled flood.
In this lush realm where humor is king,
Every plant dances, ready to spring!

Lanterns of the Dawn

As dawn breaks, the lanterns sway,
Drunk fireflies dance the night away.
A parrot squawks, "It's way too bright!"
While turtles hide, clutching real tight.

Coconuts roll, like balls of fun,
While monkeys plot to sabotage the sun.
"Hey you, lizard, don't you peek!"
Whispers from the rooster as he squeaks.

A iguana slips on morning dew,
And lands right in a puddle too.
"Nice cannonball!" the frogs all croak,
As the sun rises, they just joke.

With each flickering light, joy begins,
In this wacky world, no second wins.
The dawn unfolds with laughter bright,
In this bizarre, colorful light.

Fragrant Paths

Down the path of blooms so wide,
A skunk winks, he feels the pride.
Lilies giggle, daisies grin,
Silly scents swirl, let's begin!

"Watch that bee! It's on a spree!"
Cried the flower with glee, oh me!
Petals sway to a funky beat,
While ants tap dance on tiny feet.

The fragrance rises up like cake,
Snakes slither on for goodness' sake.
"Want a puff?" coos a dandelion,
As bees all buzz, a twist of lion.

Laughter echoes, bright and sweet,
In this world, we dance on feet.
Grab a flower, shake your head,
Join the fun, and eat some spread!

Serenity Beneath the Mango Trees

Under mango trees, oh what a sight,
Where squirrels argue over fruit in flight.
With every drop, they call and chant,
"Catch it, dude!" as they laugh and prance.

A sloth drapes down, a sleepy grin,
"Mango madness? Count me in!"
A parrot shouts, "Let's have a feast!"
Banner-waving, they joyfully feast.

The breeze rolls in with a gentle tease,
Making fun of sleepy bees.
"Hey, hurry up!" the leaves all shout,
As slumbering creatures dance about.

Underneath the branches wide,
The buzz of laughter can't subside.
With fruits and friends, the time will glow,
In haphazard joy, they steal the show!

Echoes of the Ocean Breeze

An ocean breeze starts to play,
With seaweed hats, the crabs ballet.
"Sink or swim?" they shout, in jest,
As fish wear glasses, feeling blessed.

Seagulls swoop with cawing tunes,
Making waves with funky swoons.
"Hey there, fish, you look so neat,
Wanna dance? Move those fins and feet!"

The tides giggle, swirling high,
While shells flip-flop with a sigh.
"Surf's up, dudes!" a starfish yells,
Echoes of laughter in sandy wells.

Sea cucumbers roll in the spray,
Chasing bubbles, hip-hip-hooray!
The ocean's whispers, a funny spree,
In this whimsical watery jubilee.

Vibrant Petals at Twilight

In a patch of hues so bright,
The flowers dance, a silly sight.
They wiggle, jiggle, twist, and sway,
As bees hum tunes at close of day.

Petals giggle in the breeze,
Dropping laughs like fallen leaves.
A clownish bloom with a big grin,
As butterflies join in their spin.

Jamboree of Colors

A rainbow spills on the green floor,
With daisies making a raucous roar.
Tomato plants wear silly hats,
While squawking birds engage in chats.

The sunbeam's laughter catches light,
While veggies play a game of kite.
Even snails join this merry spree,
With floppy shells and glee like thee.

The Secret Oasis

Hidden well beneath the trees,
A party starts with joyful ease.
Cactus plays the bongo drums,
While lizards dance and wiggle tums.

Secret laughter fills the air,
With ferns twirling without a care.
A hammock jokes with swinging flair,
"Don't sleep, or you might lose your hair!"

Dance of the Butterflies

Flapping wings in vibrant flight,
Flutter by with pure delight.
They wear pajamas, polka-dotted,
As they spin, we feel quite clotted.

A caterpillar starts to cheer,
With jokes that make the crowd draw near.
"Why did the flower get a date?
Because it bloomed and felt so great!"

Sunbeams and Shadows

In the rays, the lizards laze,
Wearing shades, they boost their craze.
The sunbathers stretch with a grin,
While ants march on, their tiny kin.

Parrots squawk, with flair they chatter,
Whiskers twitch, in sun they flatter.
A monkey swings on a loose vine,
While I sip juice, feeling just fine.

Symphony of the Wild

Tune confused, frogs sing a song,
Bees buzz loud, all day long.
Palm fronds wave with a gentle tease,
Loud cicadas add to the breeze.

Squirrels dance on branches high,
Chasing tails as clouds drift by.
A sneaky snake with graceful flair,
Tries to join the wild affair.

Silk-Smooth Petals

Flowers bloom in colors bright,
Bees get lost in the morning light.
Butterflies flutter, not a care,
While I trip on roots, unaware.

A toad hops in a fancy suit,
Jumping high, wearing a boot.
Petals giggle, playfully shush,
As I find my way in a rush.

Tropical Reverie

Coconuts fall, watch your head,
As crickets play hide and seek instead.
A watermelon laughs, oh what a sight,
Splashing juice with pure delight.

Pineapples dance in the cool shade,
Everyone's here for the serenade.
Laughing vines, a silly game,
In this paradise, all are same.

The Secret Life of Vines

In the corner, a vine does sway,
It naps all night and plays all day.
Swinging on branches, feeling so free,
Hiding from folks, just a leaf on a spree.

At twilight it giggles, oh what a sight,
Telling the flowers, 'We'll dance tonight!'
With each little twist, a sneaky romance,
The garden's a stage for a leafy dance.

Canvas of Color in the Understory

Painted by petals, a splash so bold,
In colors of laughter, a sight to behold.
The daisies play tricks, chasing bees round,
While sulky ferns pout, hardly making a sound.

A chameleon chuckles, blending in fast,
With every new hue, it's a color blast!
Under the shade, where the mischief feels right,
Nature's a painter, delighting in sight.

A Tapestry Woven with Nature's Thread

In the garden's embrace, a quilt made of leaves,
Sewn with giggles, it dances and weaves.
A spider spins stories, a web on a high,
'Come join the party!' it croons to the sky.

Bright butterflies flutter, fashionably late,
'We're the VIPs at this floral fête!'
Each flower a joke, a pun in disguise,
Laughter erupts when the sun starts to rise.

Birds of Paradise in Flight

High above, the birds take wing,
With beaks like trumpets, they herald the spring.
Flapping and flitting, a comedic sight,
Chasing their shadows in pure delight.

With a squawk and a caw, they dive and they twirl,
While squirrels below spin in dizzying whirl.
'Catch us if you can!' they cheekily tease,
In the grand aerial ballet amongst the trees.

The Fragrance of Joy

Beneath the sun, a flower grins,
Its petals dance, where laughter spins.
A bee, confused, wears shades of black,
He swirls around, then takes a nap.

With every scent, a giggle blooms,
The garden teems with silly tunes.
A monkey swings from vine to tree,
He steals a fruit and laughs with glee.

In every nook, a joke is told,
From tiny ants to buds so bold.
The fragrance lifts, a playful tease,
Come join the fun; just mind the bees!

Spirals of Light

Sunbeams twist like ribbons bright,
They tickle leaves with pure delight.
A parrot squawks, he loves to chat,
While chasing shadows, what of that?

The orchids giggle, swaying light,
They play a game of hide and fright.
A lizard slips, all twist and twirl,
He blushes green, gives curls a whirl.

In spirals bold, the laughter grows,
The sun dips low, a warm red glow.
With every twist, a grin takes flight,
In this wild world, all feels just right!

Blossom on the Wind

A petal flies, oh what a prank,
It flutters down, a colorful tank.
A cat leaps up in joyous chase,
Too slow, it lands and shows its grace.

The breeze sings tunes of happy days,
As flowers nod in carefree ways.
A gnome in green, tipsy and round,
He spins, then tumbles to the ground.

The joy of spring, it tickles toes,
As daisies bloom in sweet repose.
With every laugh that drifts and flows,
Life's simple bliss is all we chose!

Underneath the Hibiscus

In the shade where colors pop,
A turtle sighs and starts to drop.
Its shell, a party hat so fine,
Throws disco moves with every line.

The hibiscus blushes, proud and bold,
It whispers secrets, tales retold.
A firefly winks, a playful spark,
Illuminates the fading dark.

With laughter echoing in the air,
The garden's vibe is light and rare.
Amidst the fun, we find our dance,
Under soft blooms, an endless chance!

Reverie in the Canopy

A parrot squawks in vibrant hues,
The monkeys dance, wearing their shoes.
Lemons roll down from trees with glee,
A squirrel sipping tea, can you believe?

The sun pops out like a cheeky grin,
As lizards bask and birds begin.
The flowers wave, they know the score,
And ants march in, demanding more!

A breeze tickles the leaves just right,
While frogs leap high, what a funny sight!
A butterfly winks from a nearby bloom,
Telling jokes that lift the gloom.

So come and frolic, take a chance,
In this wild scene, join in the dance.
Where laughter grows like vines on trees,
In this funny world, you'll feel at ease.

Heartbeats of the Jungle

A toucan honks, what a noisy feat,
While zebras jive on four left feet.
The sloths just chuckle, taking their time,
As hippos join in, keeping the rhyme.

The vines hang low, like a limbo bar,
While curious monkeys swing from afar.
The parrots squawk jokes in lively tone,
While mockingbirds steal the show, full-blown.

A chorus of frogs sings off-key,
While squirrels hide nuts, what a spree!
Giggling flowers spread pollen wide,
In this jungle fun, it's a wild ride.

Join the fest, don't be a grump,
Dance with the trees, feel your heart thump.
In this jungle beat, where giggles start,
You'll find the rhythm deep in your heart.

Flourish of Enchantment

In this world where the wild things play,
The lizards run disco every day.
With twinkling eyes and glittering scales,
They jive to the tune of rustling trails.

Sunflowers giggle, spinning around,
As breezy surprises float off the ground.
Fruit flies hold parties, what a delight,
In the shade where the mischief ignites.

A chameleon changes to match the fun,
While grasshoppers hop, not ready to run.
The bananas slip, oh what a mess!
Even the daisies can't help but confess.

So lift your spirits, join this spree,
In this enchanting realm, wild and free.
With laughter blooming, so bright and bold,
This whimsical world welcomes the bold.

Vistas of Verdance

In the heart of green, where giggles sprout,
The sunbeams dance, there's no doubt.
With mushrooms grinning on every log,
And sleepy tortoises sharing a smog.

The air is ripe with laughter's tune,
As chubby bunnies waltz by the moon.
The vines entwine like a dance of fate,
Every creature, jubilant, can't wait.

Coconuts drop as they crack a smile,
While fish take selfies in a nearby isle.
The toads recite poems in rhymes absurd,
To woo the flowers, it's quite the word.

So travelers come, lose all your cares,
In these vivid sights, laughter shares.
Among the greens, a whimsical play,
In this charming realm, let's laugh away!

Oasis of Dreams

In a paradise so bright and gay,
Palm trees dance and sway all day.
A monkey swings with a cheeky grin,
As a toucan tries to mimic him.

Laughter echoes through the leaves,
As insects wear little capes and thieves.
A parrot yells, "You lost your shoe!"
While a sloth debates what he should do.

Under sunbeams that sneak and creep,
Bugs hold parties, they never sleep.
With sprightly frogs that leap and croak,
They tell jokes that make the lilies choke.

So here in this space, let your worries float,
In silly hats, we'll dance and gloat.
For in this funhouse of flora and whim,
Every moment's a laugh at the edge of a brim.

Flora's Embrace

Daisies dressed in bright pink wraps,
Tell the tropics where they're at.
A butterfly sneezes, causing a scene,
While sunflowers giggle, bright and keen.

Lily pads join in the merry fun,
Doing cartwheels under the hot sun.
A wandering bee lost in a dance,
Starts a trend, oh what a chance!

The grasses sway with bubbly tunes,
While cactus plants wear silly balloons.
A lizard in glasses plays a guitar,
"Let's make this party known near and far!"

In this embrace where laughter blooms,
Frogs and snails make up the rooms.
Each petal whispers with a chuckle or two,
In this playful realm just waiting for you.

Beneath a Floral Arc

Beneath a canopy of vibrant hues,
A snail wears shades—what a curious muse!
A crab in a tux, looking quite grand,
Sips coconut water, feeling so planned.

Through vines that twist like funny jokes,
The flowers sprout and add more hoaxes.
They gossip about the bees' funny hats,
And wonder why frogs have such chubby spats.

A butterfly DJ spins some fun tunes,
While monkeys go wild, howling at moons.
With a twirl and a leap, they join the dance,
Making the lavender sway in a trance.

So gather 'round and shed your cares,
Join this long line of quirky affairs.
A floral arc for all to see,
A wacky world where we all can be!

Watercolor Whispers

Water splashes in hues of glee,
As fish in bow ties swim with esprit.
The dragonflies wear polka-dot suits,
Making waves, oh what silly roots!

Here, the frogs throw fancy soirees,
With lattes brewed in tropical ways.
A raccoon serves snacks with a wink,
While orchids giggle, provoking a pink.

The sun dips low, creating a show,
Where colors bubble and bubbles glow.
The wind joins in with cheeky purrs,
As petals prance, spreading bright blurs.

From fragrant blooms to harmonic chords,
Everything laughs in sync, no awards!
In watercolor whispers, fun can unfurl,
Creating mischief in this wondrous world.

Beneath the Canopy's Embrace

A monkey swung with flair, oh what a sight,
He dropped a mango, oh what a fright!
Parrots squawked gossip, feathers in a tussle,
While we laughed with the breeze, feeling the hustle.

The lizards danced on leaves, quite a show,
As frogs croaked their tunes, enjoying the flow.
We sipped on smoothies, sweet and so bright,
Got sticky with fruit, what a messy delight!

Whimsy Among the Frangipanis

The blooms smell like candy, oh what a tease,
While butterflies flirt with a playful breeze.
A lizard on a branch, takes a bold leap,
Into a patch of flowers, making us weep!

We tried to take selfies, but the bees had a say,
Buzzing around us, stealing the day.
Our hats flew away, caught in a gust,
Laughing together, as we tumbled with trust!

The Melodies of Morning Dew

Morning whispers soft, like a gentle song,
With sleepy-eyed critters, all singing along.
A cockatoo yawned, and a kid laughed loud,
Echoes of joy, drifting out of the crowd.

The dew danced on petals, twinkling in sun,
As we chased after giggles, oh what fun!
A squirrel stole a donut, running away fast,
While we nibbled our snacks, hoping it would last!

Retreat to Rippling Waters

By the stream we frolicked, in the midday sun,
A frog played hopscotch; oh, such a run!
With splashes of laughter, we joined in the game,
As fish swam and giggled, oh what a claim!

We built boats of leaves, floated them wide,
Only to watch them sink, in the slip and slide.
A crab stole our sandwiches, scuttling away,
Leaving us in stitches, at the end of the day!

Renewal in Nature's Arms

In the shade of a bigleaf tree,
A parrot's squawk, quite the spree.
Frogs in suits with tiny ties,
Dance along as the sun hits the skies.

Butterflies wear polka dots bright,
Chasing each other with all of their might.
Sipping nectar, they twirl and spin,
While ants in a line try hard to fit in.

In this paradise, laughter swells,
As crickets share their funny tales.
Snakes in shades of emerald green,
Slither through the leafy scene.

A warm breeze sings a silly song,
As all the critters sing along.
Here, on this vibrant, lush stage,
Nature's humor is all the rage.

Captured by Color

Sunflowers wear big, cheesy grins,
Their heads bobbing as the fun begins.
Petunias gossip with a juicy flair,
While bees in tuxedos float through the air.

Cacti in sombreros, standing so tall,
Throw a fiesta, it's a free-for-all!
While daisies toss confetti to the breeze,
Playing hide-and-seek with buzzing bees.

Brilliant blooms in a colorful tease,
Pretend to be tall, yet they giggle with ease.
Orchids dress up in a royal gown,
Comically waltzing with nature's crown.

Poppies challenge the wind to a race,
While laughing lilies join in the chase.
Jesters of nature, a vibrant crew,
This place is alive with every hue!

Whims of Wisteria

Wisteria swings on a chandelier vine,
Throwing parties, feeling divine.
Bumblebees buzz to a catchy beat,
As flowers do the cha-cha on the street.

Hummingbirds wear tiny sun hats,
Zooming in like real acrobats.
Snails in slow motion like to strut,
While flocks of finches are ready to cut.

The sun pokes through, a golden light,
Making every color seem just right.
With petals speaking secrets to the air,
It's a carnival, humor everywhere!

In this realm where laughter blooms,
And silliness fills the fragrant rooms,
Where life is fresh and joyful anew,
Nature's court jesters always break through.

Petal-Soft Promises

In the sun, the butterflies dance,
Wearing gowns of silk by chance.
Bees are buzzing with delight,
Chasing flowers from left to right.

Lizards lounge upon the stone,
Sipping sun like it's their own.
Silly squirrels drop their nuts,
With a clatter that surely cuts!

Cacti wave from their dry place,
Saying, "Hurry, it's a race!"
Yet I stroll with steady grace,
In this wild, whimsical space.

A parrot squawks, "What's the fuss?"
Grins and giggles come from us.
In the chaos, smiles take flight,
Petal-soft, it feels just right.

The Last Orchid's Song

In the shade, the orchids bloom,
They whisper secrets in the gloom.
One last song, they softly croon,
Wishing mischief 'neath the moon.

A monkey swings from vine to vine,
Laughing at the old pine line.
With a flourish, he steals the scene,
As flowers giggle, feeling queen.

Snails in tuxedos glide with flair,
While frogs create a jazz affair.
The petals vibrate in delight,
Joy spills forth in sheer starlight.

As dawn breaks, the magic flows,
With skittish shadows, laughter grows.
A curtain call for all to sing,
In this orchestra of spring.

Swaying to Nature's Rhythm

Bamboo sways, a funky beat,
While palm fronds tap their leafy feet.
The sun shines bright, a golden show,
As critters join, a wild congo.

Giggling frogs jump all around,
Making music without a sound.
While crickets play their twilight tune,
Rabbits dance beneath the moon.

A rainbow parrot, bright and bold,
Tells jokes from the stories told.
As flowers twirl in colors spry,
Raising petals to the sky.

So let's groove, and let us sway,
In the splashy sun of day.
With laughter shared, the world's a stage,
Nature's party, youthful rage.

Colors of the Rain

When the rain falls, it paints the air,
With splashes bright, a canvas rare.
Dancing drops on leaves and blooms,
Creating music in the rooms.

A chameleon, sly and quick,
Changes hues, a colorful trick.
While puddles form, they laugh and cheer,
Splashing merrily, never fear!

Umbrellas bloom like flowers bold,
In a garden where joy unfolds.
The little ones jump, twirl, and spin,
While the plants drink from the playful din.

As the skies clear, the sun peeks out,
With rainbows painted, there's no doubt.
In this canvas, life's a game,
Framed in colors, never the same.

The Dance of Exotic Blooms

In the shade of a mango tree,
A parrot slipped on a bee.
He flapped, he squawked, oh what a sight,
As he tried to take off in flight.

Banana peels lay all around,
Slipping the cats, oh what a sound!
With every twist, they tumble and roll,
Who knew fruit could take such a toll?

Pineapples wear their crowns with glee,
While coconuts giggle, 'Look at me!'
Flowers dance in the warm soft breeze,
Wiggling their petals, oh what a tease!

Laughing lizards race to the beat,
Chasing butterflies, oh, what a treat!
In a world where humor blooms bright,
We laugh till the stars twinkle at night.

Under the Canopy of Dreams

Beneath leaves, the shadows prance,
A snail in a slow, romantic dance.
He waves to the bugs, all dressed in style,
As if every beetle could walk a mile.

Caterpillars munch on leaves with flair,
Sipping on dew, without a care.
'How many salads can one bug eat?'
They ponder aloud, it's quite the feat!

A butterfly lands on a sleepy frog,
He croaks out a tune like a casual hog.
The flowers giggle, the vines applaud,
Nature's humor—a little odd!

With every rustle, a chuckle escapes,
Laughter echoes through the green shapes.
In this haven where dreams take flight,
Even the stars join the night's delight.

Sanctuary of Sunlit Petals

Petals of colors, a wild parade,
Ticklish breezes make laughter cascade.
A sunflower grins, tipping its hat,
Inviting the bees for a quick chit-chat.

A rabbit hops by, with a wink and a hop,
He's got a bouquet, "Hey, take a swap!"
Forget-me-nots giggle in shades of blue,
While daisies dance, in their best debut.

Silly frogs croak their favorite tunes,
While dragonflies sparkle like tiny balloons.
The sun plays hide and seek all day,
As laughter bounces in the playful sway.

Each petal here tells a funny story,
Of grace and slip-ups, and moments of glory.
In every blossom, there's joy to unearth,
Nature's own laughter, a cause for mirth.

A Symphony of Fragrant Air

With scents so rich, the flowers conspire,
A nose full of joy, oh what a choir!
Every whiff a note in perfume's song,
Together they dance, all summer long.

Lime trees chuckle, offering zest,
While mangoes boast, 'We're simply the best!'
A coconut rolls, he's lost his way,
Considered a jester, they laugh and play.

Petunias twirl in their vibrant dress,
Jasmine sneezes—oh dear, what a mess!
The air is filled with giggles and cheer,
As nature conducts her symphony here.

So come, join the fun at this fragrant fair,
Where every petal has jokes to share.
In the breezy delight of colors that blend,
Laughter and joy truly never end.

The Call of the Foliage

In the shade of the palm, I found a seat,
A lizard in flip-flops, dancing on his feet.
Parrots squawk gossip, loud as can be,
A coconut drops, hitting my knee.

The flowers all giggle, in colors so bright,
The sun's playing peek-a-boo, oh what a sight!
Monkeys throw coconuts, just for a laugh,
While I sip my drink, on a shady path.

Bees buzz with rhythm, joining the play,
They wiggle and wiggle, in a funny ballet.
The breeze plays the trumpet, in rustling leaves,
Nature's a circus, or so it believes.

Under the moon's glow, the critters parade,
With fireflies glowing, like stars that we've made.
In this vibrant chaos, I find my glee,
In the charming antics of flora and spree.

A Canvas of Leaves

A canvas of green, with splashes of hue,
Painted by nature, oh what's she up to?
The orchids are laughing, their petals all frill,
While a snail with a suitcase climbs up the hill.

The hibiscus looks puzzled, with a smirk on its face,
Sipping on nectar, in a flowery race.
A chameleon's wardrobe changes with flair,
He's dazzled by choices, too many to wear.

In this world of whimsy, where legends unfold,
The daisies are gossiping, secrets retold.
A butterfly flits, with a wink and a tease,
"Join the bouquet, it's a party, if you please!"

With scents of bright fruit in the warm breezes' sweep,
I chuckle at nature, awake from her sleep.
Each leaf tells a story, each plant has a joke,
In this silly ol' patch, I dance and I poke.

Soft Significance

In a patch of tall grass, I take my rest,
A grasshopper leaps, finding bugs to jest.
The daisies wear hats, tipping to one side,
As I try not to giggle, they bloom with pride.

A snail inching slowly, thinks he's a racecar,
While ants march in line, oh how bizarre!
With flowers as chatterboxes, watch them all fine,
Debating who'll win in tonight's garden dine.

I point to a bee, who's lost in a trance,
In circles he buzzes, though there's no dance.
Laughter erupts, from a vine's gentle sway,
As if to say, "Join us, don't just delay!"

With laughter and light, in this soft little nook,
Nature's giggles and chuckles, it's all on the hook.
In this lively corner, where silliness rings,
I find my delight in the joy that it brings.

Gatherings by the Fruit Trees

Under the fruit trees, all friends come in,
With mangoes and laughter, let the fun begin!
A parrot tries yoga, in tree pose so grand,
While a raccoon juggles, with fruit in each hand.

The figs drop like marbles, in a game gone wrong,
As laughter erupts in a hilarious song.
A squirrel on roller skates zips to and fro,
With the peach pits as trophies, their skills on show.

In a circle of bananas, jokes are exchanged,
Sparkling with giggles, everybody's changed.
The watermelon slices are plotting a prank,
Hiding behind leaves, in a giggly flank.

As dusk falls softly, when the fireflies glow,
Stories of escapades begin to flow.
Underneath the fruit trees, with friends all around,
In this merry gathering, pure joy can be found.

The Garden of Forgotten Fantasies

In a patch of weeds so wild and free,
Grew a banana that dreamed of being a tree.
It'd sway and dance in a breeze so light,
Sighing, 'Oh, what a splendid sight!'

A cabbage rolled down, it took quite a trip,
Declaring itself a long-lost ship.
With sailors of radishes, bold and brave,
They set sail in search of a veggie wave.

A cheerful tomato in a bright red coat,
Started a band for the beetroot's float.
They played all night under the shining moon,
Songs of the garden in a funny tune.

As sunflowers twisted their heads in glee,
To the wacky tunes of the veggie spree.
Each petal and leaf danced with delight,
In the garden of dreams, oh, what a night!

Nectar and Nectarines

In the shade of a peach, a sneaky bee hummed,
Who dared to admit, 'I might just be plumbed!'
With nectar so sweet, they all formed a queue,
Sipping sunshine, giggling at dew.

A quirky lime tried to call out, 'Hey,
Let's start a party; we'll dance all day!'
With oranges juggling, a catchy parade,
Citrus chaos, all joyfully made.

The nectarines whispered to ripe cherries nearby,
'Not to worry; let's not be shy!
We'll trade in our peels for a sparkly crown,
And rule over fruits in this glorious town!'

As night fell soft with a twinkle and wink,
The fruits sang together, a merry old link.
In this fruity fiesta so vibrant and sweet,
Laughter kept echoing, a rhythmic heartbeat!

Shadows of Silhouetted Flora

In the shady plots where the daisies play,
The shadows turn funny, in a whimsical way.
A cactus wore shades, looking cool and bright,
Cracking jokes with a fern, 'Is it day or night?'

The violets giggled, just hiding their hues,
While talking of plants and their quirky news.
A daffodil claimed it could dance like a star,
But stumbled on pebbles, oh dear, how bizarre!

A lazy sunflower stretched wide and tall,
Said, 'Why should I move when I can just sprawl?'
The shadows laughed low, with a soft, gentle tease,
'Just reach for the light, it's a whimsical breeze!'

Underneath the moon, the laughter did swell,
As shadows played tricks, oh, what a spell!
In the dance of the night, where whimsies align,
A garden of giggles—a scene so divine!

Crescendo of Crimson Orchids

In a corner of vibrance, the orchids began,
Plots of pure mischief, each one had a plan.
With petals so bold, they strutted their stuff,
Their laugh echoed loudly, 'Oh, we're more than enough!'

A ruby-red bloom wanted to sing,
While bouncing around like a floral spring.
It crooned to the daisies, dancing in tune,
As fireflies flickered; oh, lovely, the croon!

The ferns whispered softly, 'Let's start a show,
A staged floral frolic, come join in the flow!'
With marigolds clapping, and lilies in cheer,
The crescendo of colors rang out loud and clear!

As night wrapped around in a silky embrace,
The blooms kept on laughing, with hugs interlaced.
In a bouquet of joy, the garden did glow,
A symphony of petals, a floral tableau!

Rays of Reflected Joy

In a patch of sun, I sit and grin,
Sipping sweet tea, where dreams begin.
Butterflies dance on a sugar breeze,
A lizard sneezes, then scurries with ease.

Jungle drums beat, but my phone's the star,
It's ringing loudly, from near or far.
Parrots gossip, with their comedy show,
While I pretend, I am in the flow.

An iguana slips, in yoga pose,
He's stretching hard, as if to doze.
A hammock swings, with nothing to prove,
I chuckle at life, it has such a groove.

Mangoes tumble down, they roll and sway,
I dodge them quickly, what a fun play!
Nature's the punchline, I''m laughing for sure,
In this silly place, worry's a bore.

Blooming Haven

Flowers gossip in colors so bright,
With bees competing for the best bite.
Petals flutter, like jokes gently shared,
Except for the cactus, he looks quite scared.

The roses blush, they're quite the flirts,
While daisies giggle in floral skirts.
A snail on a trellis, takes a slow dance,
I laugh at his pace, he's in a trance.

Lizards drop by for a tea party grand,
They serve their own dish, it's sand on hand!
Giggling frogs leap, with splashes so bold,
Their humor's infectious, let the tale unfold.

The sun sets fast, sparks laughter anew,
As fireflies join in, as if on cue.
In this quirky place, where joy takes flight,
Every moment's a joke, shining so bright.

Mysteries in the Breeze

The wind whispers secrets, in giggles and sighs,
A raccoon smirks, with mischief in his eyes.
Bamboo sways wildly, a dance to behold,
While chameleons prank in colors so bold.

Hidden in leaves, there's a squirrel in red,
He's plotting my snacks, that rascal ahead.
A peacock struts, with a tail like a dream,
While I sip my punch, feeling light as a beam.

Clouds above chuckle, as shadows take flight,
Tickling the grass till it giggles at night.
Unseen creatures wiggle, with rhythm so rare,
Our laughter connected, like roots laid bare.

In this wild world, where joy is the key,
I tip my hat to the wise old tree.
He nods in approval, with leaves full of cheer,
In this dance of delight, we've nothing to fear.

Essence of Sunshine

Golden rays sprinkle, like jellybeans,
While I dodge puddles, that contain weird scenes.
Bananas hang low, with a wink and a cheer,
As fruits play card games, they're quite the dear.

The sunflowers giggle, keep watch of the sky,
With their silly hats, they're aiming high.
A breeze brings the laughter from far and wide,
While I roll in the grass, full of joy and pride.

A parrot jokes, with a pirate's charade,
While sunbeams dance, in a playful parade.
With every gust, there's a tickle and tease,
As fountains burst forth and we jump with ease.

Even the shadows get swept in the fun,
As laughter lingers, never will it shun.
In this radiant realm, where smiles are spun,
Life blooms in color, under the bright sun.

The Mango Moonrise

In the evening sun, mangoes glow,
With sticky fingers, we put on a show.
The bananas giggle, the coconuts roll,
As the moon comes up, we're on a stroll.

Laughter erupts, a pineapple fumbles,
We chase after fruits, avoiding our tumbles.
A parrot squawks jokes, oh what a scene,
Dancing with laughter, it's quite the routine!

The stars sprinkle laughter, we drink from coconuts,
Twirling on grass, we forget all our ruts.
Mangoes collide with a coconut's head,
Who knew fruit fights could be this widespread!

Under the mango moon's radiant light,
We giggle and joke, what a hilarious sight.
Each fruit has a story, with each laugh we share,
In this sweet paradise, we float without care.

Silhouettes at Sundown

As the sun dips low, shadows start to play,
We lost our beach ball, oh what a dismay!
Turtles turn to spectators, caught in between,
While crabs dance the cha-cha, in a quirky scene.

Sunscreen stains cover our daring dives,
Flipping in laughter as our clumsy thrive.
The sunset whispers, "Now don't make a fuss,"
Then drops a bright orange like a ripened bus!

Fish jump and splash, joining our fun,
While we chase beach treasures under the sun.
Seagulls throw shade, causing comic delays,
Creating a symphony of silly displays!

With silhouettes stretching beneath the bright sky,
We cheer our mishaps, oh my, oh my!
As colors pop out in a vibrant array,
We'll remember this laughter long after the day.

Lullabies of the Lotus

On lily pads soft, we make our own tunes,
Croaking frogs join in, beneath the fat moons.
The lotus is swaying, a whimsical queen,
With petals that giggle, a sight so serene.

Each ripple of laughter sends dragonflies twirling,
While fish share their secrets, in water they're swirling.
We dream of big feasts, of bugs on a leaf,
The frogs croak in chorus, but we can't find the chief!

In this lush serenade, we tiptoe and sway,
With tiny bug orchestras in full display.
The crickets all chuckle, the dragonflies zoom,
Offering sweet laughs as we dance in the bloom.

So join the sweet whispers of this floral domain,
Let the lullabies carry you far from mundane.
With giggles and grace, we'll drift through the night,
In this dreamy oasis, everything feels right.

Enigma of the Orchid

Amidst the butterflies, an orchid perplexes,
With colors so bold, it sends out complex texts.
A bee buzzes close, "What's for dinner tonight?"
While orchids respond, "Oh, just here for the flight!"

They hide their sweet nectar, keep secrets confined,
As we scratch our heads, in bright colors entwined.
What goes on in petals? We laugh and we muse,
In this riddle of flowers, we sip our fruit brews.

Silly garden gnomes are up to some art,
With potted plants dancing, they've stole the show start!
We giggle at vines that twist and they shout,
While orchids snicker, "What's this fuss about?"

As mystery deepens, we twirl and we cheer,
Spinning in circles, shedding all fear.
Together we ponder, "What's next in our script?"
In this lovely conundrum, we'll never feel stripped!

Mosaic of Nature's Splendor

In corners bright with pots amiss,
A gnome just tripped on a big chrysanthemum.
The parrot squawked, "This isn't bliss!"
While munching on a cucumber.

The sunflowers swayed in silly dance,
As bees buzzed by with a belly laugh.
A squirrel took its chance for a prance,
And stole the gardener's half-eaten gaff.

Lemons dropped like comets, so bold,
And oranges rolled with a citrus cheer.
The mulch proclaimed, "This is pure gold!"
While worms grinned from ear to ear.

A chameleon on a branch did tease,
Changing colors like it's dress-up time.
Lizards lounged on sun-warmed leaves,
Claiming sun as their prime-time mime.

Escape to the Wildflower Realm

A butterfly slipped on flower tea,
And tumbled right onto a bumblebee.
The daisies giggled, quite carefree,
As pollen flew like confetti spree.

A fox with a hat made of daisies bright,
Attempted to dance but fell with a thud.
A rabbit rolled over, what a sight!
And landed right in a garden mud.

The violets whispered, "Don't be so shy!"
As frogs croaked jokes from their lily pad throne.
"Would you like some flies?" was their sly reply,
To all who watched their comedy zone.

With ladybugs sharing tales of old,
And grasshoppers hopping in jiggy groove,
In this wild realm, life's a jolly hold,
The laughter of nature speaks to improve.

Echoes of the Ocean's Breath

A crab in a shell did a wiggly dance,
While seagulls cawed in a comical court.
Starfish laughed at their own lack of chance,
To join the beach party and bask in rapport.

The waves did giggle as they crashed ashore,
Tickling toes of sun-kissed teens.
A beach ball bounced like a silly score,
And landed in an ice-cream machine!

A dolphin leapt with a splashy kick,
While fish planned pranks with a wink and a swirl.
They tossed a net just for a quick flick,
Caught in a whirlwind, oh what a whirl!

Shells scattered jokes like fortune's glee,
While mermaids sang in a jazzy way.
"Just float along, come dance with me!"
As sea cucumbers dwindled to sway.

Sunlight Filtering Through Emerald

Under leaves, a party was underway,
As shadows danced with a twinkling gaze.
Frogs with crowns called, "Join our ballet!"
And tree trunks played games, lost in a haze.

The sunlight poked with a ticklish beam,
Turning petals into glittery pals.
A lizard dreamed of a dragon-themed dream,
While ants marched with their tiny pals.

Pine cones crafted hats with flair,
On squirrels who posed like kings on the vine.
"Who wore it best?" they'd giggle and stare,
While robins sang out, "It's your time to shine!"

A breeze carried laughter in soft, sweet notes,
As all gathered for a festive parade.
This vibrant circus, where joy promotes,
In the canopy's cradle, rhythmically swayed.

Arboreal Secrets

In a jungle so dense, a squirrel took flight,
He wore tiny goggles, a most comical sight.
With acorns for fuel, he zoomed through the trees,
Chasing after fairies, shouting, "Catch me if you please!"

The toucan, a judge with a wig made of leaves,
Declared the best dancers should win their reprieves.
But one monkey slipped on a banana peel,
And everyone burst out laughing, what a deal!

Rhapsody of the Rain

Raindrops were playing a symphony sweet,
As frogs donned top hats and shuffled their feet.
A parrot in bow tie led the grand show,
While snails joined in, moving quite slow.

Each splash on the puddle began a big dance,
With insects in chorus, they seized the chance.
The grass sang a pitchy, hilarious tune,
As butterflies twirled beneath the soft moon.

The Garden of Dawn

The sun peeked in with a wink and a grin,
A party of blooms stretched, ready to spin.
The daisies competed in who could sway best,
While the roses shook petals, declaring a jest.

A caterpillar claimed he was quite the champ,
But stumbled right over a very large lamp.
The plants all erupted in giggles and glee,
As he spun around like a child with no fee.

Starlit Blossom

Under the stars, the moon gave a nod,
As critters convened with a whimsical plod.
A hedgehog in shades played the bongo with flair,
While fireflies twinkled, completing the air.

The night was alive with a wacky parade,
Of dancing cockroaches, a grand masquerade.
But one silly bat got tangled in a vine,
And the laughter that followed was simply divine!

www.ingramcontent.com/pod-product-compliance
Lightning Source LLC
Chambersburg PA
CBHW052221090526
44585CB00015BA/1432